1,000,000 Books

are available to read at

www.ForgottenBooks.com

Read online
Download PDF
Purchase in print

ISBN 978-1-334-47136-0
PIBN 10736639

This book is a reproduction of an important historical work. Forgotten Books uses state-of-the-art technology to digitally reconstruct the work, preserving the original format whilst repairing imperfections present in the aged copy. In rare cases, an imperfection in the original, such as a blemish or missing page, may be replicated in our edition. We do, however, repair the vast majority of imperfections successfully; any imperfections that remain are intentionally left to preserve the state of such historical works.

Forgotten Books is a registered trademark of FB &c Ltd.
Copyright © 2018 FB &c Ltd.
FB &c Ltd, Dalton House, 60 Windsor Avenue, London, SW19 2RR.
Company number 08720141. Registered in England and Wales.

For support please visit www.forgottenbooks.com

1 MONTH OF FREE READING

at
www.ForgottenBooks.com

By purchasing this book you are eligible for one month membership to ForgottenBooks.com, giving you unlimited access to our entire collection of over 1,000,000 titles via our web site and mobile apps.

To claim your free month visit:
www.forgottenbooks.com/free736639

* Offer is valid for 45 days from date of purchase. Terms and conditions apply.

English
Français
Deutsche
Italiano
Español
Português

www.forgottenbooks.com

Mythology Photography **Fiction**
Fishing Christianity **Art** Cooking
Essays Buddhism Freemasonry
Medicine **Biology** Music **Ancient Egypt** Evolution Carpentry Physics
Dance Geology **Mathematics** Fitness
Shakespeare **Folklore** Yoga Marketing
Confidence Immortality Biographies
Poetry **Psychology** Witchcraft
Electronics Chemistry History **Law**
Accounting **Philosophy** Anthropology
Alchemy Drama Quantum Mechanics
Atheism Sexual Health **Ancient History**
Entrepreneurship Languages Sport
Paleontology Needlework Islam
Metaphysics Investment Archaeology
Parenting Statistics Criminology
Motivational

REDUCTION OF TAXES BY ACTS OF CONGRESS.

The following exhibits the **estimated reduction** of annual internal taxation and customs duties under the laws mentioned:

Act of July 13, 1866	$65,000,000 00
Act of March 2, 1867	40,000,000 00
Act of February 3, 1868	28,000,000 00
Acts of March 1 and July 20, 1868	45,000,000 00
Act of July 14, 1870	78,848,827 33
Acts of May 1 and June 6, 1872	51,823,761 38

Time will not permit me to go further into details.

The great republican party, besides saving the Republic whose destruction was sought not only by the rebellion but by all the crowned heads of the world, (save the Czar of Russia,) has shown itself capable of adjusting the delicate task of reconstruction, and to-day, but eleven years since the close of the war, every State is fully represented on this floor.

This great party has given freedom and citizenship to all its people. Every one of its great fundamental principles form a part of the Constitution and are the accepted principles of all parties. As a practical business-like party it has reduced the *per capita* expenses (less war expenses) twenty-five cents below what it was when it assumed governmental power.

Since this party assumed control it has reduced the average annual cost of clerks by the sum of $175 each and they do 50 per cent. more work.

The losses on the collections and disbursements of the public funds have greatly decreased.

The system of checks and balances in the keeping governmental accounts is vastly improved.

The character and capacity of Government officials are greatly bettered.

The Government credit which stood at 12 per cent. interest on its loans is now reduced to 4½ per cent.

It has gradually year by year since the war reduced expenses and taxation.

It has paid nearly $600,000,000 of the public debt in the last eleven years.

It has provided for every obligation of the Government, including the sinking fund.

It has reduced the annual interest burden by $45,000,000. It has pensioned the brave soldiers who fought to save the country.

It may not at all times have done the wisest thing, and some of its officials have been dishonest and corrupt.

But it has a glorious record, one that causes its adherents to rejoice and be glad that they share its glories.

To put against this party, the democracy proposes economy and reform, when they have not shown a single characteristic that entitles them to the appellation of reformers. Under this cry they will try to have the people forget that the complete fruition of reconstruction is not yet an accomplished fact.

They want us to forget that democratic success means the practical loss of the rights of citizenship to the colored people of the South. With democratic success these rights will exist only in name.

They want the people to forget that hundreds of millions of war claims are to be paid, dependent upon their success.

They want the people to forget the many schemes of southern plunder that will be accomplished facts with their ascendency.

The people who saved the Republic are ever watchful and alert. They who have sacrificed so much to make the old flag an emblem of freedom and glory will not trust gentlemen with power who sought to trail it in the dust and substitute in its place the stars and bars, until they manifest a spirit that will assure them that the great principles fought for and won are secure in their hands.

The spectacle of a people turning over the destinies of a great country to the very men who sought to destroy it will not be witnessed for four years to come at least.

The following statement shows reductions and postponements finally agreed upon by both Houses:

Statement showing the reduction and postponements of appropriations as finally agreed upon.

Pension		$466,500 00
Military Academy		74,675 00
Consular and diplomatic		216,405 50
Fortifications		535,000 00
Legislative		4,528,276 93
River and harbor		1,643,517 50
Deficiencies		3,886,975 62
Post-office		2,408,707 00
Naval		4,280,651 00
Indians		690,437 53
Army		1,946,662 10
Sundry civil		10,286,444 62
		29,944,352 86
Deduct deficiency		3,886,975 62
		26,057,377 24
Deduct Court of Claims	$2,000,000 00	
Indefinite for assay office	500,000 00	
Indefinite	500,000 00	
		3,000,000 00
		23,057,377 24
Deduct also—		
Centennial	$1,500,000 00	
Washington Monument	200,000 00	
Pennsylvania avenue	200,000 00	
Fortifications	200,000 00	
New York post-office	227,000 00	
Agricultural Reports	130,000 00	
		2,457,000 00
Actual reduction and postponement		20,600,377 24

[FROM CONGRESSIONAL RECORD.]

Repeal of the Resumption Law.

SPEECH

OF

HON. JAMES A. GARFIELD,

OF OHIO,

DELIVERED IN THE

HOUSE OF REPRESENTATIVES,

Friday, November 16, 1877.

—:o:—

"Our own history has recorded for our instruction enough, and more than enough, of the demoralizing tendency, the injustice and the intolerable oppression on the virtuous and well disposed, of a degraded paper currency, authorized by law, or in any way countenanced by Government."

WEBSTER'S SPEECHES, Vol. II, p. 81.
[Ed. 1835.]

—:o:—

WASHINGTON:
R. O. POLKINHORN, PRINTER,
1877.

SPEECH.

———o———

The House having under consideration the bill (H. R. No. 805) to repeal the third section of the Act, entitled "An Act for the resumption of Specie Payments"—

Mr. GARFIELD said:

We are engaged in a debate which has lasted in the Anglo-Saxon world for more than two centuries; and hardly any phase of it to which we have listened in the course of the last week is new. Hardly a proposition has been heard on either side which was not made one hundred and eighty years ago in England, and almost a hundred years ago in the United States. So singularly does history repeat itself.

That man makes a vital mistake who judges of truth in relation to financial affairs from the changing phases of public opinion. He might as well stand on the shore of the Bay of Fundy and, from the ebb and flow of a single tide, attempt to determine the general level of the sea, as to stand on this floor and, from the current of public opinion in any one debate, judge of the general level of the public mind. It is only when long spaces along the shore of the sea are taken into the account that the grand level is found, from which all heights and depths are measured. And it is only when long spaces of time are considered that we find at last that level of public opinion which we call the general judgment of mankind. From the turbulent ebb and flow of the public opinion to-day I appeal to that settled judgment of mankind on the subject-matter of this debate.

In the short time which is allotted to me I invite the attention of gentlemen, who do me the honor to listen, to a very remarkable fact. I suppose it will be admitted on all hands that 1860 was a year of unusual business prosperity in the United States. It was at a time when the bounties of Providence were scattered with a liberal hand over the face of our Republic. It was a time when all classes of our community were well and profitably employed. It was a time of peace; the apprehension of our great civil war had not yet seized the minds of our people. Great crops North and South, great general prosperity marked the era.

If one thing was settled above all other questions of financial policy in the American mind at that time, it was this, that the only sound, safe, trustworthy standard of value was coin of standard weight and fineness, or a paper currency convertible into coin at the will of the holder. That was and had been for several generations the almost unanimous opinion of the American people. It is true there was here and there a theorist, dreaming of the philosopher's stone, dreaming of a time when paper money, which he worshipped as a kind of fetish, would be crowned as a god; but those dreamers were so few in number that they made no ripple on the current of public thought, and their theories formed no part of public opinion. The opinion of 1860-'61 was the aggregated result of the opinions of all the foremost Americans who have left their record upon this subject.

I make this statement without fear of contradiction, because I have carefully examined the list of illustrious names and the records they have left behind them. No man ever sat in the chair of Washington as President of the United States who has left on record any word that favors inconvertible paper money as a safe standard of value. Every President who has left a record on the subject has spoken without qualification in favor of the doctrine I have announced. No man ever sat in the chair of the Secretary of the Treasury of the United States who, if he has spoken at all on the subject, has not left on record an opinion equally strong, from Hamilton down to the days of the distinguished father of my colleague [Mr. EWING] and to the present moment. The general judgment of all men who deserve to be called the leaders of American thought, ought to be considered worth something in an American House of Representatives on the discussion of a great topic like this.

What happened to cause a departure from this general level of public opinion? Every man knows the history. War, the imperious necessities of war, led the men of 1861-'62 to depart from the doctrine of the fathers; but they did not depart from it as a matter of choice, but compelled by overmastering necessity. Every man in the Senate and House of 1862, who voted for the greenback law, announced that he did it with the greatest possible reluctance and with the gravest apprehension for the result. Every man who spoke on the subject, from Thaddeus Stevens to the humblest member in this House, and from Fessenden to the humblest Senator, warned his country against the dangers that might follow, and pledged his honor that at the earliest possible moment the country should be brought back to the old, safe, established doctrine of the fathers.

When they made the law creating the greenbacks they incorporated into its essential provisions the most solemn pledge men could devise, that they would return to the doctrines of the fathers. The very law that created the greenback provided for its redemption and retirement; and whenever the necessities of war required an additional issue, new guarantees and new limitations were put upon the new issues to insure their ultimate redemption. They were issued upon the fundamental condition that the number should be so limited forever that under the law of contracts the courts might enforce their sanctions. The men of 1862 knew the dangers from sad experience in our history; and, like Ulysses, lashed themselves to the mast of public credit when they embarked upon the stormy and boisterous sea of inflated paper money, that they might not be beguiled by the siren song that would be sung to them when they were afloat on the wild waves.

But the times have changed; new men are on deck; men who have forgotten the old pledges; and now only twelve years have passed (for as late as 1865 this House, with but six dissenting votes, resolved again to stand by the old ways and bring the country back to sound money)—only twelve years have passed, and what do we find? We find a group of theorists and doctrinaires who look upon the wisdom of the fathers as foolishness. We find some who advocate what they call "absolute money;" who declare that a piece of paper stamped a "dollar" is a dollar; that gold and silver are a part of the barbarism of the past, which ought to be forever abandoned. We hear them declaring that resumption is a delusion and a snare. We hear them declaring that the eras of prosperity are the eras of paper money. They point us to all times of inflation as periods of blessing to the people and prosperity to business; and they ask us no more to vex their ears with any allusion to the old standard, the money of the Constitution. Let the wild swarm of financial literature that has sprung into life within the last twelve years witness how widely and how far we have drifted. We have lost our old moorings, have thrown overboard our old compass; we sail by alien stars, looking not for the haven, but are afloat on a harborless sea.

To those who do not believe in keeping the promise of the nation at any time, I make no argument to-day; but to those of our brethren in this House who believe that at some time or another we ought to return to the ways of the fathers, to the money of the Constitution—to those I address myself. There are many among them who believe that some time or other we can resume specie payments, but who believe that to-day or in 1879 it is impossible or if possible inexpedient; that from such an attempt evils will arise to the country greater than the benefits; and therefore they join in seeking the repeal of the act of 1875. I have no doubt they regret to throw their influence with those men who do not believe in resuming at all. To them I say, before the final vote is taken, "Let us reason together."

I want it remembered in the outset, that the greenback currency was and is—so known in the courts and so known everywhere—a forced loan, a loan forced by the Government upon its Army and upon its other creditors to meet the great emergencies of the war; and the primary fact connected with every greenback is that it is a promise to pay. Those who believe in resumption, intend that some time or other the nation shall make good the promise.

Now what are the obstacles to resumption, in accordance with the law we have passed? The first great obstacle stated by gentlemen who have argued the question is this: that we have not enough currency in the country for its business and that some measure of contraction will be likely to attend the further execution of the provisions of the resumption law. Before I enter directly upon that objection I desire to state a fact for the consideration of those who hear me. In that prosperous era of 1860, when there was free banking in most of the States, and the banks were pushing all the currency they could into circulation without limit, there were just two hundred and seven millions of paper currency, and that was the largest volume that this country had ever known.

Mr. BUCKNER. Will the gentleman allow me to make a statement on that point?

Mr. GARFIELD. If my time would allow me, I would be happy to yield to the gentleman.

Mr. BUCKNER. I wish to say that Secretary Cobb reported in 1857 that we had two hundred and fifteen millions of circulation in paper and two hundred and seventy five millions in coin in gold and silver.

Mr. GARFIELD. I will say to the gentleman from Missouri that not only years ago, but again recently I have gone through the reports and made the most careful estimate of which I have been capable, and I beg to state that two hundred and seven millions is the recognized settled amount for 1860. It is true that for a few months just previous to the panic of 1857 the volume of paper money did reach two hundred and fifteen millions; but that was wholly exceptional. In no year of prosperity had the volume been so great as in 1860.

Now, nobody estimates that the amount of coin in the country in 1860 was more than $250,000,000. The received estimate is two hundred millions. Add that sum to the two hundred and seven millions of paper circulation, and you have four hundred and seven millions of currency, paper and silver and gold. How much have we to-day? This day, or rather on the first day of this month, we had seven hundred and twenty seven millions of greenbacks, bank notes, fractional currency, and fractional silver; and if you add the nine millions of copper and nickel money now outstanding, it makes a present volume of seven hundred and thirty-six millions of currency, counting no gold whatever, although the Pacific coast uses a large amount.

Now, I put it to the judgment of this House if, under free banking in 1860, four hundred and seven millions was the limit of possible currency that could be kept in circulation, how can it be said that almost twice that amount is needed and is hardly enough for the wants of 1877? Have the laws of value changed in seventeen years? Gentlemen who assert a dearth of currency at the present time must point out the new elements in our fiscal affairs that require three hundred and twenty millions more money than was needed in 1860.

Mr. HARRISON. Will the gentleman allow me to ask him a question?

Mr. GARFIELD. I am speaking in the time of another gentleman; but if the House will extend my time I will be glad to have as much debate as gentlemen please.

The SPEAKER. The gentleman from Ohio declines to yield.

Mr. GARFIELD. No theory of currency that existed in 1860 can justify the volume now outstanding. Either our laws of trade, our laws of value, our laws of exchange, have been utterly reversed, or the currency of to-day is in excess of the legitimate wants of trade. But I admit freely that no Congress is wise enough to determine how much currency the country needs. There never was a body of men wise enough to do that. The volume of currency needed depends upon laws that are higher than Congress and higher than governments. One thing only legislation can do. It can determine the quality of the money of the country. The laws of trade alone can determine its quantity.

In connection with this view, we are met by the distinguished gentleman from Pennsylvania [Mr. KELLEY] with two historical references on which he greatly relies in opposing resumption. The first is his reference to France. Follow France, says the honorable gentleman from Pennsylvania, follow France, and see how she poured out her volumes of paper money, and by it survived a great crisis and maintained her business prosperity. O, that the gentleman and those who vote with him would follow France! I gladly follow up his allusion to France. As a proof that we have not enough money, he notices the fact that France has always used more money than either the United States or England. I admit it. But does the gentleman not know that the traditions and habits of France are as unlike those of England and the United States as those of any two nations of the world can be in regard to the use of money? I say to the gentleman that in France, banking as an instrument of trade is almost unknown. There are no banks in France except the bank of France itself. The government has been trying for twenty years to establish branches in all the eighty-nine departments, and thus far only fifty-six branches have been organized. Our national, State, and private banks number nearly ten thousand. The habits of the French people are not adapted to the use of banks as instruments of exchange. All the deposits in all the savings-banks of France are not equal to the deposits in the savings-banks of New York City alone. It is the frequent complaint of Americans who make purchases in Paris that the merchants will not accept drafts even on the Bank of France.

Victor Bonnet, a recent French writer, says:

> The use of deposits, bank accounts. and checks is still in its infancy in this country. They are very little used even in the great cities, while in the rest of France they are completely unknown. It is, however, to be hoped that they will be more employed hereafter, and that here, as in England and the United States, payments will be more generally made through the medium of bankers and by transfers in account-current. If this should be the case, we shall economize both in the use of specie and of bank-notes, for it is to be observed that the use of bank-notes does not reach its fullest development except in countries where the keeping of bank accounts is unusual, as is evident by comparing France in this respect with England.
>
> M. Pinard, manager of the Comptoir d'Escompte, testified before the commission of inquiry that the greatest efforts had been made by that institution to induce French merchants and shopkeepers to adopt English habits in respect to the use of checks and the keeping of bank accounts, but in vain; their prejudices were invincible. "It was no use reasoning with them; they would not do it, because they would not."

So long as the business of their country is thus done hand to hand by the use of cash, they need a much greater volume of money in proportion to their business than England or the United States.

How is it in England? Statistics which no man will gainsay, show that 95 per cent. of all the great mercantile transactions of England are done by drafts, checks, and commercial bills, and only 5 per cent, by the actual use of cash. The great business of commerce and trade is done by drafts and bills. Money is now only the small change of commerce. And how is it in this country? We have adopted the habits of England, and not of France, in this regard. In 1871, when I was chairman of the Committee on Banking and Currency, I asked the Comptroller of the Currency to issue an order naming fifty-two banks which were to make an analysis of their receipts. I selected three groups: the first was the city banks; not, however, the clearing-house banks, but the great city banks not in the clearing-house associations. The second consisted of banks in cities of the size of Toledo and Dayton, in the State of Ohio. In the third group, if I may coin a word, I selected the "countriest" banks, the smallest that could be found, at points away from railroads and telegraphs.

The order was that those banks should analyze all their receipts for six consecutive days, putting into one list all that can be called cash either coin, greenbacks, bank-notes, or coupons, and into the other list all drafts, checks, or commercial bills. What was the result? During those six days, $157,000,000 were received over the counters of the fifty-two banks; and of that amount, $19,370,000—12 per cent. only in cash—and 88 per cent. of that vast amount, representing every grade of business, was in checks, drafts, and commercial bills. Does a country that transacts its business in that way need as much currency afloat among the people as a country like France, without banks, without savings institutions, and whose people keep their money in hoards?

I remember in reading one of the novels of Dumas, when an officer of the French army sent home an agent to run his farm, he loaded him down with silver enough to conduct the business for a year; there was no thought of giving him credit in a bank; but of locking in the till at the beginning of the year enough coin to do the business of the year. So much for the difference between the habits of France and those of Anglo Saxon countries.

Let us now consider the conduct of France during and since the German war. In July, 1870, the year before the war began, the Bank of France had outstanding $251,000,000 of paper circulation and held in its vaults $229,000,000 of coin. When the war broke out, they were compelled immediately to issue more paper and to make it a legal-tender They took pattern by us in their necessity, and issued paper until on the 19th of November, 1873, four years ago next Monday, they had $602,000,000 of paper issued by the Bank of France, while the coin in the bank was reduced to $146,000,000.

But the moment their great war was over, they did what I commend to the gentleman from Pennsylvania, [Mr. KELLEY:] they commenced to reduce their paper circulation; and in one year reduced it almost $100,000,000, and increased the coin reserve $120,000,000. In the year 1876, they had pushed into circulation $200,000,000 of coin, and retired nearly all their small notes. They are at this moment within fifty days of resumption of specie payments. Under their law, fifty days from to-day France will again come into the illustrious line of nations who maintain a sound currency. I commend to the eloquent gentleman from Pennsylvania [Mr. KELLEY] the example of France.

Before leaving this point it is worth while to notice the fact that France has not yielded to the paper-money doctrines which find so much favor here. One of her ablest financial writers, Victor Bonnet, writing in July, 1873, says:

It is difficult to say to what point we can reduce the credit circulation; but whatever point that may be, a paper currency will never be sound unless it is based on a very considerable reserve of specie, nor unless it is accompanied by a favorable state of the exchanges.
The fact that we have lately had a paper circulation of 3,000,000,000 francs without depreciation, does not militate against this assertion. This result accomplished by means of a large reserve of specie and a favorable state of the foreign exchanges. It succeeded perfectly, and we may fairly assert that, financially speaking, it saved France. Nevertheless, we ran great risks. If trade had not revived immediately after the commune; if foreigners had not shown confidence in the future of France by subscribing to our loans; if we had been obliged to export a large amount of specie to pay the Prussian indemnity; in a word, if the exchanges had continued very unfavorable to us, as they were for a brief period at the end of 1871, our paper money would very quickly have fallen in value, and its downward progress would have been rapid, much more rapid than the increase in its amount. Fortunately for us, the contrary of all this has happened; but let us not draw any false inferences for the future from this happy concurrence of circumstances. We may be sure that the principles which regulate a credit currency are precisely the same in 1874 as they were prior to 1870, and that a condition of legal tender and suspended specie payments is always a misfortune. We submit to it when it is inevitable, but we should hasten to get out of it as soon as we have the means.

But the gentleman has found something in the example of England which he uses to bolster up his opposition to resumption. There is nothing more remarkable than the sudden popularity of certain writers who till very lately were unknown as authorities on finance. About ten years ago, when I tried to make a careful study of these questions, I came across a pamphlet which I thought, at the time, the most remarkably absurd document I had ever read—a pamphlet published under the sanction of the name of Sir Archibald Alison, entitled "England in 1815 and 1845; or, a Sufficient and a Contracted Currency." I took pains to make a careful synopsis of it, and as the new doctrines of money sprang up in Congress I wondered that nobody quoted from Sir Archibald Alison; but I have heard Alison *ad nauseam* during the last four or five years. Who is Sir Archibald Alison? What American can take pride in quoting as an authority a man whose hatred of republican institutions was deeper and stronger than any other English tory; a man in whose heart there was never a throb of sympathy with popular institutions. No man who fills an important place in English history has less credit than he on questions of finance.

Let me give a specimen of the financial wisdom of Sir Archibald Alison, of whom the gentleman from Pennsylvania [Mr. KELLEY] is so enamored. On pages 2 and 3 of the pamphlet to which I have referred that writer says:

> The eighteen years of war between 1797 and 1815 were, as all the world knows, the most glorious and, taken as a whole, the most prosperous that Great Britain has ever known. * * * Never has a prosperity so universal and un-heard of pervaded every department of the empire.

He then enumerates the evidences of this prosperity, and prominent among them is this:

> While the revenue raised by taxation was but £21,000,000 in 1793, it had reached £72,040,000 in 1815; and the total expenditures from taxes and loans had reached £117,000,000 it 1815!

Happy people, whose burdens of taxation were quadrupled in eighteen years and whose expenses, consumed in war, exceeded their revenues by the sum of $225,000,000 in gold!

This is the kind of financial authority that gentlemen now parade with so much satisfaction in the Congress of the United States.

Another man, a Mr. Doubleday, is also drafted into the service. I do not find that any penny-a-liner in England, much less any great journalist, has ever deigned to answer, in an English paper, the twaddle of that writer. He is, however, just now very popular with certain gentlemen in the United States, and he has been flung at us during the last six or seven years, until it has seemed as though tomahawks were flying through the air, with "Doubleday" inscribed on their blades.

Mr. HARRISON. Will the gentleman allow me to ask him a question here——

[Cries of "Order!" "Oh, no!" from many members.]

The SPEAKER. Objection is made, and the gentleman will proceed without interruption.

Mr. GARFIELD. Waiving, however, all that may be said in regard to the merits of these two writers, I say in reply that the overwhelming and fixed opinion of England is that the cash-resumption act of 1819 was a blessing, and not a curse, and that the evils which England suffered from 1821 to 1826 did not arise from the resumption of cash payments. I appeal to every great writer of acknowledged character in England for the truth of this position. I ask gentlemen to read the eighth chapter of the second book of Miss Martineau's History of the Peace, where the case is admirably stated. I appeal also to the opinion of Parliament itself, especially to the House of Commons, which is as sensitive an index of public opinion as England knows. When they were within about eighteen mouths of resumption of specie payments, a motion was made, like the motion of my colleague. [Mr. EWING,] that the resumption-act be repealed or modified, because it was producing distress. And a number of gentlemen in the House of Commons made speeches of the same spirit as those which we have heard here within the past week. The distress among the people, the crippling of business, the alarm of the merchantile classes, all were paraded in the House of Commons, and were answered by those knights of finance whose names have become illustrious in English history. And at the end of a long debate on that proposition, on the 11th of April, 1821, a vote was taken, and the proposition was rejected by a vote of 141 to 27. In other words, by a vote of 141 to 27, the House of Commons resolved that their act for the resumption of specie payments was not causing distress, ough not to be repealed, and ought not to be modified except to make it more effective. As a matter of fact, it was so modified as to allow resumption to take place much sooner than was provided in the act of 1819.

But this was not enough. On the 11th of June, 1822, a Mr. Western moved for the appointment of a committee to inquire into the effect of the resumption law, and charged that it had caused a violent contraction of the currency and an injury to the business of the country. Again the subject was fully debated, and the arguments against the resumption act were completely answered. By a vote of 192 to 30 the motion of Mr. Western was rejected; and the Commons resolved that they would not alter the standard of gold or silver, in fineness, weight, or denomination. Surely the House of Commons must be assumed to know something of the condition of England, as much at least as Mr. Alison, who wrote upon the subject a quarter of a century afterwards.

Still, gentlemen tell us that the great distress in England was caused by the resumption act. I commend those gentlemen to such great writers as Tooke, who in his History of Prices has gone over this ground most thoroughly and ably. He says it was the corn law which produced the great evils from which England suffered in those years.

A law had been passed to prevent the price of wheat from falling below eighty shillings per quarter, by prohibiting all foreign importations whenever the price fell below that figure. In other words, England proposed to build a Chinese wall around the island so as to make wheat one of the most profitable crops for her farmers. Stimulated by that law, the agriculturalists of England undertook the growing of wheat on a scale before unknown. And when they had expended millions in reclaiming waste lands and sowing an unusual breadth of wheat, they found their own harvest and the colonial importations had flooded the market and lowered the price, and bankrupted thousands of English farmers. In spite of the law, wheat went down to forty-seven shillings and nine pence per quarter, and brought great distress upon the agricultural population.

That this fall in the price of wheat was not caused by the resumption act is conclusively shown by the fact that the three great harvests of 1820, 1821, and 1822 were general throughout Europe, and on the Continent, the price of wheat declined almost as much as in England itself.

In 1822 a committee of the House of Commons was appointed to inquire into all the causes of the distress. I have read that report in full, and there is not a word in it that attributes any part of the distress to the resumption act of 1819; but the causes given are those which I have named.

Mr. Speaker, I was amazed at my friend from Pennsylvania [Mr. KELLEY] presenting a table here which he found in somebody's atlas, a table giving the amount of circulating notes in England during different years from 1818 to 1826, and opposite each year the word "prosperity" or the word "distress." This table has been referred to by gentlemen on the other side as proof that the resumption act of England produced the distress of 1825. If gentlemen will look at their own table they will find a conclusive answer to their proposition. The gentleman from Pennsylvania said a day or two ago in answer to a question, that the cash-payment act went into effect in 1823. In that he was mistaken; it went into effect in 1821. But suppose he was correct; his table shows that the years 1824 and 1825 were years of great prosperity and speculation. Those two years that followed the date of resumption as given by him are put down in his own table as years of "great prosperity and speculation." Does that prove that distress was produced by the resumption act? The fact is that the great speculation during the apparent prosperity of 1825 was the beginning and the cause of the tremendous crisis that struck England in the latter part of 1825, and prostrated its business again. This is the testimony of her foremost writers.

Before quitting this point I beg leave at once to put myself in the category to which the gentleman from Pennsylvania assigned the late Secretary of the Treasury, Hugh McCulloch. He read three lines from a paper of Mr. McCulloch in the North American Review and said it was an example of astonishing ignorance or astonishing mendacity. What was the statement denounced as so ignorant or so mendacious? It was that every great crisis in this country has been preceded by an enlargement of paper circulation. I affirm that to be true, and I challenge any man to controvert it. It was true in England always. It has been true in this country always. We had a great crisis in 1797; another in 1817; another in 1837; another in 1857; and our last in 1873—almost exactly twenty years apart.

These crises are periodic, and return as the result of causes springing up among the mass of our business people; and they have all been preceded by overtrading, speculation, an enlargement of credits, an undue expansion of the instruments of credit; and they have all resulted in the same sad uniformity of misery that has followed their culmination.

[Here the hammer fell.]

MANY MEMBERS. Go on!

Mr. CONGER. I ask unanimous consent that the gentleman from Ohio be allowed to proceed.

The SPEAKER. The gentleman from Michigan asks consent that the gentleman from Ohio have his time extended. Is there objection?

Mr. DOUGLAS. I object.

Mr. FORT. I certainly desire that the gentleman's time be extended, but I apprehend that many gentlemen are desirous to have the time of this debate extended. Unless that is done I shall object.

Mr. DOUGLAS. I withdraw my objection.

Mr. ATKINS. There is no objection on this side.

The SPEAKER. Does the gentleman from Illinois object?

Mr. FORT. In connection with the extension of the gentleman's time, I ask that the time of this debate be extended.

The SPEAKER. The same power that extends an increase of time to the gentleman can extend the debate.

Mr. FORT. I desire to have the gentleman's time extended; I am very much pleased to hear him speak; but the time assigned for this debate is now well-nigh run, and it seems to me——

The SPEAKER. If the gentleman from Illinois desires the time extended, the Chair will consider it as a withdrawal of the objection.

Mr. STEPHENS, of Georgia. I propose that the time for debate generally be extended just so long as the additional time which the gentleman from Ohio wishes to occupy.

Mr. DOUGLAS. I want it distinctly understood that I withdraw my objection to the etexnsion; but I will remark at the same time that I shall object to any further extensions of time.

The SPEAKER. The Chair understood the gentleman to withdraw his objection.

Mr. BUCKNER. Let us understand how long the gentleman from Ohio wishes to occupy the floor. I have no sort of objection.

Mr. GARFIELD. I think about fifteen or twenty minutes.

Mr. TOWNSEND, of Illinois. Unless it is agreed that the time for general debate on the bill shall be extended, I object.

The SPEAKER. The gentleman cannot object qualifiedly.

Mr. GARFIELD. I am very much obliged to the House for its kindness.

I now proceed to notice the second point has been made in favor of this bill. It is assumed that specie payment will injure the debtor class of this country, and thereby oppress the poor; in other words, that the enforcement of the resumption law will oppress the poor and increase the riches of the rich. It is assumed that the laboring men are in debt, and that the rich men constitute the creditor class. I deny this proposition *in toto*. I affirm that the vast majority of the creditors of this country are the poor people; that the vast majority of the debtors of this country are the well-to-do people; in fact, people who are moderately rich.

As a matter of fact, the poor man, the laboring man, cannot get heavily in debt. He has not the security to offer. Men lend their money on security; and, in the very nature of the case, poor men can borrow but little. What, then, do poor men do with their small earnings? When a man has earned, out of his hard work, a hundred dollars more than he needs for current expenses, he reasons thus: "I cannot go into business with a hundred dollars; I cannot embark in trade; but, as I work, I want my money to work." And so he puts his small gains where they will earn something. He lends his money to a wealthier neighbor or puts it into a savings-bank. There were in the United States on the 1st of November, 1876, forty-four hundred and seventy-five savings-banks and private banks of deposits; and their deposits amounted to $1,377,000,000, almost three-fourths the amount of our national debt. Over two and a half millions of the citizens of the United States were depositors. In some States the deposits did not average more than $250 each. The great mass of the depositors are men and women of small means—laborers, widows, and orphans. They are the lenders of this enormous aggregate. The savings-banks, as their agents, lend it to whom? Not to the laboring poor, but to business men who wish to enlarge their business beyond their capital. Speculators sometimes borrow it. But in the main, well-to-do business men borrow these hoardings. Thus the poor lend to the rich.

Gentlemen assail the bondholders of the country as the rich men who oppress the poor. Do they know how vast an amount of the public securities are held by poor people? I took occasion, a few years since, to ask the officers of a bank in one of the counties of my district, a rural district, to show me the number of holders and amounts held of United States bonds on which they collected the interest. The total amount was $416,000. And how many people held them? One hundred and ninety-six. Of these, just eight men held from $15,000 to $20,000 each; the other one hundred and eighty-eight ranged from $50 up to $2,500. I found in that list, fifteen orphan children and sixty widows, who had a little left them from their fathers' or husbands' estates, and had made the nation their guardian. And I found one hundred and twenty-one laborers, mechanics, ministers, men of slender means, who had kept what they had and put it in the hands of the United States that it might be safe. And they were the "bloated bondholders," against whom so much eloquence is fulminated in this House.

There is another way in which poor men dispose of their money. A man says, I can keep my wife and babies from starving while I live and have my health; but if I die they may be compelled to go over the hill to the poorhouse; and, agonized by that thought, he saves of his hard earnings enough to take out and keep alive a small life-insurance policy, so that, if he dies, there may be something left, provided the insurance company to which he intrusts his money is honest enough to keep its pledges. And how many men do you think have done that in the United States? I do not know the number for the whole country; but I do know this, that from a late report of the insurance commissioners of the State of New York, it appears that the companies doing business in that State had 774.625 policies in force, and the face value of these policies was $1,922,000,000. I find, by looking over the returns, that in my State there are 55,000 policies outstanding; in Pennsylvania, 74,000; in Maine, 17,000; in Maryland, 25,000, and in the State of New York, 160,090. There are, of course, some rich men insured in these companies; but the majority are poor people; for the policies do not average more than $2,200 each. What is done with the assets of these companies, which amount to $445,000,000? They are loaned out. Here again the creditor class is the poor, and the insurance companies are the agents of the poor to lend their money for them. It would be dishonorable for congress to legislate either for the debtor class or for the creditor class alone. We ought to legislate for the whole country. But when gentlemen attempt to manufacture sentiment against the resumption act, by saying it will help the rich and hurt the poor, they are overwhelmingly answered by the facts.

Suppose you undo the work that Congress has attempted—to resume specie payment—what will result? You will depreciate the value of the greenback. Suppose it falls ten cents on the dollar. You will have destroyed ten per cent. of the value of every deposit in the savings banks, ten per cent. of every life-insurance policy and fire-insurance policy, of every pension to the soldier, and of every day's wages of every laborer in the nation.

In the census of 1870 it was estimated that on any given day there were $120,000,000 due to the laborers for their unpaid wages. That is a small estimate. Let the greenback dollar come down 10 per cent. and you take $12,000,000 from the men who have already earned it. In the name of every interest connected with the poor man, I denounce this effort to prevent resumption. Daniel Webster never uttered a greater truth in finance than when he said that of all contrivances to cheat the laboring-classses of mankind none was so effective as that which deluded them with irredeemable paper money. The rich can take care of themselves; but the dead-weight of all the fluctuation and loss falls ultimately on the poor man who has only his day's work to sell.

I admit that in the passage from peace to war there was a great loss to one class of the community, to the creditors: and in the return to the basis of peace some loss to debtors was inevitable. This injustice was unavoidable. The loss and gain did not fall upon the same people. The evil could not be balanced nor adjusted. The debtors of 1862-'65 are not the debtors of 1877. The most competent judges declare that the average life of private debts in the United States is not more than two years. Of course, obligations may be renewed, but the average life of private debts in this country is not more than two years. Now, we have already gone two years on the road to resumption, and the country has been adjusting itself to the new condition of things. The people have expected resumption, and have already discounted most of the hardships and sufferings incident to the change. The agony is almost over; and if we now embark again upon the open sea, we lose all that has been gained and plunge the country into the necessity of trying once more same the boisterous ocean, with all its perils and uncertainties. I speak the deepest convictions of my mind and heart when I say that, should this resumption act be repealed and no effectual substitute be put in its place, the day is not far distant when all of us, looking back on this time from the depth of the evils which are sure to result, will regret, with all our power to regret, the day when we again let loose the dangers of inflation upon the country.

Gentlemen speak of the years of high prices as years of prosperity. It is true there was a kind of prosperity in the days of high prices; but do not gentlemen know that war prices cannot be kept up forever? Nothing but the extraordinary calamities of war can produce such prices as we knew from 1865 to 1870. To our foreign and domestic markets was added the war market. War sat like a grim monster swallowing up the accumulated wealth of the country. More than a million men were taken out of the ranks of the producers and added to the ranks of consumers,; and prices went up; but does anybody dream that these prices could be kept up forever, after the soldiers were mustered out and the war had closed and business had begun to resume its normal level of peace? O, no, gentlemen, it was inevitable that the country must come down from the level of war prices; and the attempt to prevent it is to fight against fate. Unless we bring ourselves steadily and surely by strong courage and the guidance of law back to resumption, we shall reach that level by a disastrous fall; but down to it we must come.

I do not undervalue the greenback or its great services to the country; but when the gentleman from Pennsylvania [Mr. KELLEY] spoke of the greenback as being the thing that put down the rebellion, I thought if 1 had been on the other side I would have said: "We had a much more liberal supply of paper money than you had; why did it not put you down? [Laughter.] Our money was better than yours in one respect, for ours set a day of resumption, which was six months after the independence of the Confederate States should be acknowledged." [Laughter.] I think, sir, that those gentlemen who are familiar with the financial history of the confederacy would not join the gentleman in his eulogy on paper currency which is cut loose from the coin standard.

Our country needs not only a national but an international currency. Let me state a fact of vast importance in this discussion. The foreign trade of this country—its exports and imports—amounts to $1,500,000,-000 in value; and every dollar of that trade must be transacted in coin. We cannot help ourselves. Every article of export we send abroad is measured by and sold for coin. Every article of import we must pay for in coin. We must translate these coin prices into our currency; and every fluctuation in the value of the greenback falls upon us and not upon the countries with which we trade. Therefore the commercial interests of America demand that the international and national value of money shall be one, so that what is a dollar in Ohio shall be a dollar the world over. Our money must be international as well as national, unless we wish to isolate this country and have no trade or commerce, or glory on the sea

The trouble with our greenback dollar is this: it has two distinct functions, one a purchasing power and the other a debt-paying power. As a debt-paying power it is equal to one hundred cents; that is, to pay an old private debt. A greenback dollar will by law discharge one hundred cents of debt. But no law can give it purchasing power in the general markets of the world, unless it represents a known standard of coin value. Now, what we want is that these two qualities of our greenback dollar shall be made equal—its debt-paying power and its general purchasing power. When these are equal, the problem of our currency is solved, and not till then.

We who defend the resumption act propose not to destroy the greenback but to dignify it, to glorify it. The law that we defend does not destroy it, but preserves its volume at $300,000,000 and makes it equal to and convertible into coin. I admit that the law is not entirely free from ambiguity. But the Secretary of the Treasury, who has the execution of the law, declares that section 3579 of the Revised Statutes is in full force, namely:

When any United States notes are returned to the Treasury, they may be reissued, from time to time, as the exigencies of the public interest may require.

Although I do not believe in keeping greenbacks as a permanent currency in the United States, although I do not myself believe in the Government becoming a permanent banker, yet I am willing for one, that, in order to prevent the shock to business which gentlemen fear, the $300,000,000 of greenbacks shall be allowed to remain in circulation at par, as long as the wants of trade show manifestly that they are needed. Now, is that a great contraction? Is it a contraction at all?

Why, gentlemen, when you have brought your greenback up two and one-half cents higher in value, you will have added to your volume of money $200,000,000 of gold coin which cannot circulate until greenbacks are brought to par. Let those who are afraid of contraction consider this fact and answer it.

Summing it all up in a word: the struggle now pending in this House is, on the one hand, to make the greenback better, and on the other, to make it worse. The resumption act is making it better every day. Repeal that act and you make it indefinitely worse. In the name of every man who wants his own when he has earned it, I demand that we do not make the wages of the poor man to shrivel in his hands after he has earned them; but that his money shall be made better and better, until the plow-holder's money shall be as good as the bond-holder's money; until our standard is one, and there is no longer one money for the rich and another for the poor.

This is the era of pacification. We believe in the pacification of the country. That is, we seek to pass out of the storm-centre of war that raged over this country so long, and enter the calm circle of peace. We believe in the equality of States, and the equality of citizens before the law. In these we have made great progress. Let us take one step further. Let us have equality of dollars before the law, so that the trinity of our political creed shall be equal States, equal men, and equal dollars throughout the Union. When these three are realized we shall have achieved the complete pacification of our country.

We are bound for three great reasons to maintain the resumption of specie payments: First, because the sanctity of the public faith requires it; second, because the material prosperity of the country demands it; and, third, because our future prosperity demands that agitation shall cease and that the country shall find a safe and permanent basis for financial peace.

The conditions are now all in our favor. The Secretary of the Treasury tells us in his report, laid upon our table this morning, that he has $66,000,000 of gold coin, unpledged for any other purpose, waiting as a reserve for the day of resumption. He is adding to that stock at the rate of $5,000,000 a month. Our surplus revenue of $35,000,000 a year, all will be added to this reserve. Foreign exchange is now in our favor. We are selling to other nations almost $200,000,000 a year more than we are buying. All these elements are with us. Our harvests are more bountiful than ever before. The nation is on the returning wave of prosperity. Everywhere business is reviving, and there is no danger except from the Congress of the United States. Here is the storm-centre; here is the point of peril. If we can pass this peril and not commit ourselves to the dangerous act now threatened, we shall soon see resumption complete.

I notice that gentlemen do not move to strike out the first section of the resumption act. Why? Two years ago my colleague, [Mr. EWING,] in his debate with Governor Woodford, laughed at silver resumption, so far as the fractional currency was concerned, as absurd and impossible.

He spurned the proposition to destroy our paper scrip, which cost but little, and replace it with silver change which had some value. He argued that every silver coin issued would be hidden away and none would go into circulation. But since that debate, silver resumption under the first section of the act is completed, except that we have not yet been able to find all of the old scrip, so lazily do the people exercise their right of redemption. But gentlemen think that now, if we resume under this section, the greenbacks will all be taken up.

Mr. EWING. Will the gentleman allow me a moment?

Mr. GARFIELD. Certainly.

Mr. EWING. In the debate with Governor Woodford in 1875 I did make the statement to which the gentleman refers. But that was before the people of this country, or, I presume, the people of the world generally, knew of the furtive and rascally act of demonetization of silver in the adoption of our Revised Statutes. It was before the immense fall of silver. It was when the silver dollar was at a high premium over the greenback dollar. Speaking from conditions then existing, and the price of silver at that time, the statement was reasonable that the fractional silver currency would be taken up and sold, and not go into general circulation.

Mr. GARFIELD. The trouble with the statement of my friend is that the fractional silver currency being 12 per cent. below the value of the silver dollar, there was not the slightest danger, at the time he speaks of, that the silver change after being issued would pass out of circulation. My friend did not believe in silver resumption until that metal became so depreciated as to be worth vastly less than paper.

Gentlemen think there is danger that the people will present all their greenbacks and demand the coin, if resumption is enforced. Let us see. Remember how slow they have been in giving up their scrip. Suppose that a farmer in one of your eastern States sells his farm for $10,000. He wants to remove to the great West. He gets ten greenbacks of the denomination of $1,000 each. This is easy to carry; he can put it his vest pocket. Do you think, as a matter of convenience, he will go to the assistant treasurer in New York and get for those greenbacks forty pounds' weight of gold coin to carry in his pockets, or, if the silver dollar should be restored, six hundred and forty pounds of silver? No, gentlemen; the moment your greenback is equal to gold, it is better than gold, for it is more convenient, and it will remain in circulation until the business of the country demands its withdrawal.

In conclusion, Mr. Speaker, if any of the substitutes offered to this bill will make resumption more safe, more certain, and will more carefully protect the business interests of the country, such amendment shall have my vote; but any measure, that takes back the promise, that gives up what we have gained, that sets us afloat on the wild waves from which we have so nearly escaped, I will oppose it to the utmost, confidently trusting to the future for the vindication of my judgment. [Applause.]

[FROM THE CONGRESSIONAL RECORD.]

THE NEW SCHEME OF AMERICAN FINANCE.

A REPLY TO HON. W. D. KELLEY.

SPEECH

OF

HON. JAMES A. GARFIELD,

OF OHIO,

"*Capital may be produced by industry and accumulated by economy; but jugglers only will propose to create it by legerdemain tricks with paper.*"—THOMAS JEFFERSON.

"*If there be, in regard to currency, one truth which the united experience of the whole commercial world has established, I had supposed it to be that emissions of paper money constituted the very worst of all conceivable species of currency.*"—HENRY CLAY.

WASHINGTON:
R. O. POLKINHORN, PRINTER.
1878.

CPSIA information can be obtained
at www.ICGtesting.com
Printed in the USA
LVHW010744291118
598533LV00024BA/1345

9 781334 471360